ADHD and Autism: What Every Parent Should Know About This

A Parent's Aid in Raising Their Children with ADHD and Autism

By: Shelley Lewis

9781634286886

PUBLISHERS NOTES

Disclaimer – Speedy Publishing LLC

This publication is intended to provide helpful and informative material. It is not intended to diagnose, treat, cure, or prevent any health problem or condition, nor is intended to replace the advice of a physician. No action should be taken solely on the contents of this book. Always consult your physician or qualified health-care professional on any matters regarding your health and before adopting any suggestions in this book or drawing inferences from it.

The author and publisher specifically disclaim all responsibility for any liability, loss or risk, personal or otherwise, which is incurred as a consequence, directly or indirectly, from the use or application of any contents of this book.

Any and all product names referenced within this book are the trademarks of their respective owners. None of these owners have sponsored, authorized, endorsed, or approved this book.

Always read all information provided by the manufacturers' product labels before using their products. The author and publisher are not responsible for claims made by manufacturers.

This book was originally printed before 2014. This is an adapted reprint by Speedy Publishing LLC with newly updated content designed to help readers with much more accurate and timely information and data.

Speedy Publishing LLC

40 E Main Street, Newark, Delaware, 19711

Contact Us: 1-888-248-4521

Website: http://www.speedypublishing.co

REPRINTED Paperback Edition: ISBN: 9781634286886

Manufactured in the United States of America

Dedication

I dedicate this book to my lovely daughter who inspired to grasp more information about ADHD/ADD to better understand her condition. May this book be useful to parents like me.

TABLE OF CONTENTS

CHAPTER 1- ADHD BY DEFINITION

Attention Deficit Hyperactivity Disorder or ADHD is a mental disorder, which approximately three to seven percent children are having. Due to this disorder children manifest the characteristic of constant behavior, loads of activity as well as often being considered disobedient.

That does not mean that the individual is being bad but the thing is they don't have control over their mental range. They go through lack of concentration because at a time they are likely to be thinking about many elements instead of one particular element.

This disorder is also found in many adults besides children. In adults, it is called Adult Attention Deficit Disorder or AADD. Among all children diagnosed with ADHD about 30 to 70 percent will carry on with their disorder through adulthood.

Adults learn to live with it and work around it and need less help. They can handle the disorder of their own and so it's harder to detect also. Yet, in many cases both children and adult may need medications for better results.

In children this disorder shows signs like inattentiveness, impulsive behavior and a constant restlessness. In adults, it is harder to diagnose but children with this disorder cannot sit still for long.

They cannot concentrate on one particular thing for a long period of time. In adults, it becomes difficult sometimes to structure their lives and to plan daily activities. They don't feel the importance to stay attentive or to stop being restless because these are not at all important problems for them.

ADHD is a disorder for which assistance of medical personnel is necessary. It can be treated but cannot be cured fully. For this disorder medication is also necessary.

They're actually three different types of ADHD; each with different symptoms. There's predominantly inattentive, predominantly hyperactive/impulsive, and the combined type. And to diagnose ADHD an individual must display at least six symptoms from very specific lists from the DSM-4 and the symptoms have to have started before the age of seven to diagnose a child.

So they also have to have clear impairment in at least two settings, such as home and school or school and work and there must be clear evidence of significantly clinical impairment in social, academic, or occupational functioning.

So there's very specific criteria that you need in order to diagnose a person with ADHD and if one is going to fall within the predominantly inattentive type they have to meet one they have to meet six of these criteria fail to pay close attention to details or make careless mistakes in school work or other activities, have difficulty sustaining attention to task or leisure activities; they may often seem not to listen when spoken to directly; they do not follow through on instructions and fail to finish school work, chores, duties; they have difficulty organizing tasks and activities; they avoid, dislike, or are reluctant to engage in tasks that require sustained mental effort; they lose things necessary for the task; they are easily distracted and are forgetful in daily activities. So if a child has six of these characteristics then they might be diagnosed with the inattentive type of ADHD.

If they are if they fidget with their hands or their feet, they squirm in their seat, they leave their seat in situations in which they're supposed to remain seated, they move excessively, they feel restless during situations in which behavior is inappropriate, they have difficulty engaging in leisure activities quietly, they often seem like they're on the go or they're driven by a motor, they talk excessively, they blurt out answers, they have difficulty awaiting their turn, they interrupt or intrude on others either in their space or verbally; if they have six of these characteristics then they can be diagnosed for the hyperactive ADHD.

It affects an estimated 2,000,000 American children, so at least one child in every US classroom can be diagnosed with ADHD. In general, boys outnumber girls with ADHD at a rate of about three to one and girls most often have the inattentive type.

ADHD is often mistaken or found occurring with other neurological, biological, and behavioral disorders. Nearly half of all children with ADHD especially boys tend to have also oppositional defiant disorder which is characterized by negative, hostile, and defiant behavior.

They may also have conduct disorder which is marked by aggression towards people and animals and destruction of property, deceitfulness, theft, and serious rule-breaking. Those are often found to co-occur with an estimated 40-percent of children with ADHD. And approximately one-fourth of children with ADHD, mostly younger children and boys, also experience anxiety and depression and at least 25-percent of children with ADHD suffer some type of communication or a learning disability. And additionally they have found a correlation between Tourettes Syndrome, which is a neurologically based disorder characterized by motor and vocal tics and ADHD only, like if you were only an ADHD person is actually quite a small percentage; so they there are quite a few other things that ADHD and other disorders are combined with.

CHAPTER 2- WHAT CAUSES ADHD AND ITS TREATMENT

It's important to realize that ADHD is not caused by dysfunctional parenting nor is it due to a lack of intelligence or discipline. Often people think that you know this child is stupid or you know they're uncontrollable but in fact that's not the case.

There is strong evidence to support the conclusion that ADHD is a biologically based disorder and recently the National Institute of Mental Health observed pet scans and showed significantly lower metabolic activity in regions of the brain controlling attention and social judgment and so therefore that also lends to the idea that it's biologically based.

Biological studies also suggest that children with ADHD have lower levels of the neurotransmitter Dopamine critical of regions of the brain, so that also lends to the idea that it's biologically based. There are other theories that suggest cigarette or alcohol and drug use during pregnancy or exposure to environmental toxins such as lead, may be linked to the development of ADHD. Research also suggests that there is a strong genetic basis to ADHD; the disorder tends to run in families.

In addition, research has shown that certain forms of genes related to the Dopamine neurotransmitter system are linked to increase likelihood of the disorder, so there are biological bases, there are possible chemical bases, you know whether it be nicotine or alcohol; there are environmental toxins that may link to ADHD; so there's quite a few possibilities as to what may lead to a child developing ADHD.

The most proven treatments are medication in combination with behavioral therapy and stimulants are the most widely used drugs for treating attention deficit hyperactivity disorder. The four most commonly used stimulants are Ritalin, Dexedrine, Adderall, and Siler, and these drugs increase the activity in parts of the brain that are under-active, which often confuses people why would we be prescribing a stimulant when the person is already hyperactive, but when you think about a drug stimulating areas of the brain that are under-active then it would make sense.

Therefore it improves attention and it reduces impulsiveness, hyperactivity, and aggressive behavior. At times anti-depressants are prescribed for people who have ADHD and sometimes those help as well and most recently the FDA has approved a non-stimulant medication called Strattera and that also has been proven to be very helpful. But every person reacts differently to treatment, so it's important to work closely and communicate openly with your physician so that you know you have the best treatment as far as medically based treatment.

It's also very important to remember the side effects of medications which include weight loss, decreased appetite, trouble sleeping, and in children sometimes a temporary slowness in growth, but however these reactions can be controlled by dosage adjustments. That's why it's always very important to talk with your physician frequently and especially as a child grows and their weight changes and their need for the medication may change, so it's very important to communicate openly with them.

And medication has been proven effective in the short-term treatment in more than 76-percent of individuals with ADHD. So medication is definitely one avenue to work and to look at treatment.

And then as far as behavioral therapies, behavioral therapy would reward positive behavior change and communicating clear expectations to those people with ADHD those things are very important. I mean the consistency where a behavioral therapy plan is delivered is very important.

It's extremely important for family members and teachers and employers to remain patient and understanding and consistent but behavioral therapy in combination with medication or even without medication have been proven highly successful.

So children with ADHD can additionally benefit from caregivers paying close attention to their progress and adapting classroom environments to accommodate to their needs and using positive reinforce(s) and where appropriate parents should talk with the school district to plan an individual educational program which is also known as IEP.

Given that so many would to a certain extent keep away from the use of stimulant medications for the healing of attention deficit hyperactivity disorder if probable, an increasing want for the growth of alternative treatments for ADD, ADHD has risen since the past twenty years.

Even though there are many products that state to help out any child with ADD or ADHD, the fact is that there are only a small amount of non medicine healing for attention deficit disorder that have in reality gone through even the easiest of medical tests. The majority of alternative healings have never been cautiously studied to find out their efficiency in the real world.

Four preferred non medicinal healings for attention deficit disorder have been studied in the real world. They are Brainwave Biofeedback training, Behavior Modification therapy, Eating or Diet Interventions, and the Nutraceutical medicines called "Extress" and "Attend".

Therapy can have helpful advantages under some situations, such as the expertise of the counselor in working with ADD or ADHD persons. A lot of counselors have little knowledge in working with these people.

"Attend" and "Extress" are superb substitutes to treatment stimulant medicines. They are very complicated procedures, engineered to achieve maximum efficiency in brain functioning in individuals going through problems with concentration, impulse control, rage, listening attentively, or hyper activity.

EEG Biofeedback training, also known as Neurofeedback is around a twenty year old technology. With the ongoing progress of faster and faster computers it has developed into a feasible alternative healing for ADD.

There is a vast amount of study on EEG Biofeedback, which you ought to go through if you are at all concerned. The EEG Spectrum is a great web site for a lot of information on this treatment alternative.

Eating plans, or diet involvements, might also have some constructive effect on persons with attention deficit hyperactivity disorder. Even though we do not feel that this involvement is as effectual as either the Attend and Extress, or EEG Biofeedback training, we do consider that every person with ADHD ought to try a diet involvement.

A lot of persons with ADD or ADHD will also be helped from nutritional supplements. The most effectual are most likely Essential Fatty Acids which are also known as Omega Oils and particular minerals like Zinc.

ADHD and Autism
The necessary fatty acids you will find present in the "Attend" nutraceutical. You also get them in Borage Oil or Flax Seed Oil. They can in addition be found in fish, and you can just give your child more of tuna fish to eat.

Chapter 3- ADHD Children Affects the Relationship in the Family

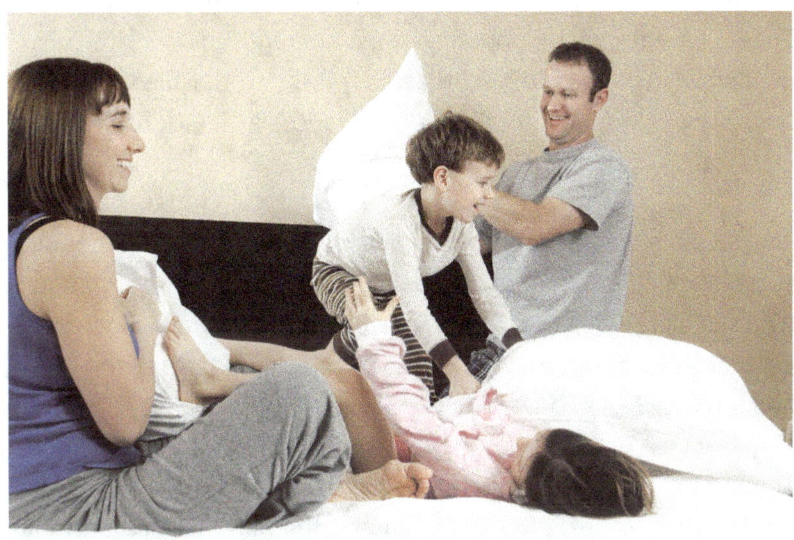

Attention Deficit Disorder usually comes with a lot of frustration and blame. Often the diagnosis happens late and so, the disease–related problems are often misunderstood.

This may result in serious emotional and mental scars when the family tries to deal with ADD–related issues. Thus, this disorder is difficult for the diseased child, the parents and the siblings.

The child who is suffering from ADD is clearly the first victim. Though these children have a strong desire to show normal behavior, their actions can be impulsive. This impulsive behavior often gets punished. Because of these punishments, these children often develop very low self-esteem.

Many times, the parents and teachers are either not aware of or do not accept that the child has a disorder and thus don't behave in a mature and conscious way. After the child has been scolded or punished for his impulsive actions, the child feels that he will never be up to the mark and meet others' expectations from him.

The next victims of ADD are obviously the parents of the child. These parents start doubting their parenting and are often incredibly frustrated. Often, these parents are ridiculed by family members, teachers and other acquaintances as if lack of discipline is the cause of their child's problem.

They begin to see their rearing habits in poor light. They sometimes start blaming each other for being excessively lenient or harsh while dealing with the child. The disagreements and arguments that result from this may put considerable strain on their marriage and relationship.

Though not apparent at first glance, siblings of the child with ADD are the next victims after the child and the parents. Like the child with ADD and the parents, they also suffer from anxiety and frustration. As the child with ADD is given so much attention by everyone, even if it is negative, they develop jealousy towards the child with ADD.

As the child with ADD can be aggressive, the siblings often suffer due to the impulsive actions of the child. Also, often the siblings are categorized in social environments and schools owing to the behavior of their brother/ sister. This all can have negative effect on the siblings.

After immediate family, cousins, uncles, aunts, grandparents etc. of the child with ADD may also be affected. Depending on how close the family is outbursts in the behavior and the discipline–related issues may be an important factor to be dealt with again and again. In extreme situations, ADD may cause rifts in the relationships.

Life ahead may be easy for a child, a teenager, or even an adult diagnosed with ADD. For somebody, just diagnosed with ADD, predicting the life in future might not be easy, as one may not know how the symptoms would continue to remain and how the problem would be affected by age. However, thankfully, as time moves on, one starts to understand how to deal with ADD more efficiently, so that it causes fewer troubles in life.

Children with ADD are usually unmindful, reckless, or may get distracted easily or may show too much of goings-on. Also, the symptoms remain mostly the same even in other age groups. However, dealing with these symptoms does improve significantly, as one gets older.

The affect ADD can have on your life is largely determined by the medication you choose for treating the disorder. You may wish to consult the doctor to give you an advice on the future effects of taking stimulants, and also the implications of other medicines. Medicines are useful in dealing with ADD, though you can also try a behavior therapy too.

There are some characteristic traits, typical of ADD that you should prepare for in your life. These may be difficulties in being attentive to details, problem in remaining still for any span of time, being fidgety, or problem in being able to stay through and complete a given task.

Nevertheless, you can do a number of things in order to deal with the behavior typically related to ADD. To become more orderly and more managed in keeping things, an organizer can prove to be quite useful. For this, you can choose from anything like the effective book calendars to the digital organizers that are quite technologically sophisticated, to personal assistants. These will keep you well ordered, provided you are well trained to use these devices so that they can remember your important information and schedules.

These routines and schedules should be used to their maximum. You will naturally be inclined to forget and be careless. So by using a proper device you will tend to behave more unlike your nature and thus make lesser mistakes. So, it is always better to use automation.

You may also wish to be a part of groups, for support, or may at least want the company of the ones like you. You may feel the need for someone to confide in, who can understand you situation well. A person with ADD could be a perfect companion since they may be able to connect with you better than any friend or a family member, since they can support you only to a limit.

Chapter 4- The Signs and Symptoms of ADHD

Diagnosis is difficult in cases of ADD because signs vary from child to child. The symptoms of the disorder may or may not be obvious.

First of all you must be clear that just because your child is hyperactive, he is not suffering from ADD. It is true that more than normal activities are a sign of ADD but not always so. But, at the same time impulsive behavior, or less than normal attention, or more than normal distraction is a sign of ADD.

Actually, distraction and lack of attention go together. An ADD suffering child will not be able to stick to his work and will not pay much attention to details and may not complete his work. Although most children are like this but those who suffer from ADD show more extremes of this behavior can go on for more than 6 months. Thus his daily work is affected.

Kids having ADD are impulsive too. They may suddenly run away from their desks to see what is happening in the other part of the room. They may even give out answers in the class even if they are not asked. His behavior may be impulsive to such extremes. It is a common trait in all ADD affected children.

These kids attach themselves to everything that is happening. They may become hypersensitive and may not be able to concentrate on anything in particular. Hence their grades are lower than usual even if they don't really have difficulties in learning anything because they don't complete their tasks. Their attention span is so short that they are incapable of completing the work allotted to them.

There is difference in behavior among the two sexes also. Boys are more active and girls are less attentive in the class. It is difficult to manage both of them and both may be unruly in behavior or aggressive and may be even abusive. Thus it becomes very difficult to control them.

But all kids differ from each other. You will never find two similar kids. Only because your child is more aggressive than others don't jump to the conclusion that he has ADD. Only a physician or a specialist can diagnose ADD.

ADD is a Learning Disability?

When we talk of the term 'learning disability' then what we generally mean is that it is a perceptual disability like other disabilities such as autism or visual processing disorder, or dyslexia auditory disability.

It should not be treated as a learning disability. Anyone who has ADD is perfectly capable of understanding and using the available information. Hence it cannot be considered as a learning disability.

ADD doesn't really obstruct the learning process although it is combined with all other disabilities most of the time. A small child who is suffering from ADD can take in the information he sees and then he can process it and even keep it in his memory just like normal human beings. The only problem is attracting his attention for long enough so that he may take in the information to begin with.

He has problems in school and also in general but this can't be treated as a disability of any kind. Once the treatment for his ADD problem starts, his performance in school shoots up. But sometimes, a person who has ADD problem might not be having any difficulty in his education at all. It is different from person to person.

But we must remember that there are other disabilities, especially, in very small preschool children, they might have problems in understanding sounds and words and may have some speech problems too.

Those kids who are of reading writing age may experience reading, writings and mathematical and spelling problems. Similarly Dyslexia, which is reading disorder, is very common among children having ADD. But it must be kept in mind that it is not necessary that all the children may have these problems.

Some difficulties may arise in ADD affected children but here there are various ways of improving the situation. Most of them are benefited by a fixed schedule, by having the same time for all the activities. They are weak in remembering things, so routine work helps them. The habit developed by repetition of activity helps them.

Similarly, if you keep things in a fixed place then they find it easier to remember it. They can even be helped by binders and planners for the activities they have to undertake. It helps them in being organized.

In class, if the teacher has an interactive attitude instead of giving a lecture then the child manages to give more attention to the work in hand and his frequency of distractions may go down.

Thus, you must remember that a child, inspire of having this disorder can grow into a successful person.

Chapter 5- ADHD is a Disease of a Phase?

When you were a kid, didn't you run about all the time for no particular cause? Didn't you continuously turn your concentration from one thing to the other? Didn't you have a tough time sitting motionless? Didn't you have a tough time concentrating on one thing, for long span of time? You were a kid and you behaved the manner in which nearly all children do.

You did not reflect about things, you simply did them since at that age, there was no thinking procedure. Nearly all children get through this stage in their early life, but science has gone ahead and told us that perhaps this action is not so normal.

Attention Deficit Disorder, how do we describe it? You would believe with all the great minds in the world that somebody would have come up with a description that suits. But that is not the case it appears that ADD is an arbitrary definition and not essentially an illness.

There is still puzzlement over who does and does not have ADD. A few associates of the mental health association had a demand to categorize any person with ADD, as having a brain deficiency.

Apparently this was as a result of the fact that the first group of ADD patients that were studied had been ill with encephalitis, which is an inflammation of the brain. This criterion is no longer valid, for the reasons that over the years, people with no brain deficiencies, have been added to the roll call of ADD.

At this time, there are two most important kinds of ADD. ADD with hyperactivity and ADD without hyperactivity. Indications of ADD plus hyperactivity are described as: can't keep on seated, restless, climbs or runs a lot, talks much, can't play peacefully and also having a tough time standing in line or waiting for their turn. A few indications of ADD without hyperactivity are, disordered, having a tough time concentrating on tasks, with no trouble getting diverted and does not appear to pay attention.

Therefore, who has ADD? The numbers by and large given are 3 to 5 percent of the people. But no one knows. Since ADD is so arbitrary, it is apparent that several who are listed as ADD, may not even fit in there.

There is still an important debate going on as to the validness of ADD. Is it genuine? A number of people say that ADD is not an illness, but a compilation of mannerisms and indications, that may possibly be generated by any number of troubles.

When you include the reality that the specialists in the field, can't even make a decision on what precisely ADD is and who precisely has it, then this only gives more credibility to those that gave a suspicion over the presence of ADD. Of course there are lots of people who consider that ADD is genuine and not just some stage a person is going through. They consider that people ought to be taken care of for their symptoms and not be anticipated to just get out of them.

CHAPTER 6- CONTRIBUTORS TO ADHD

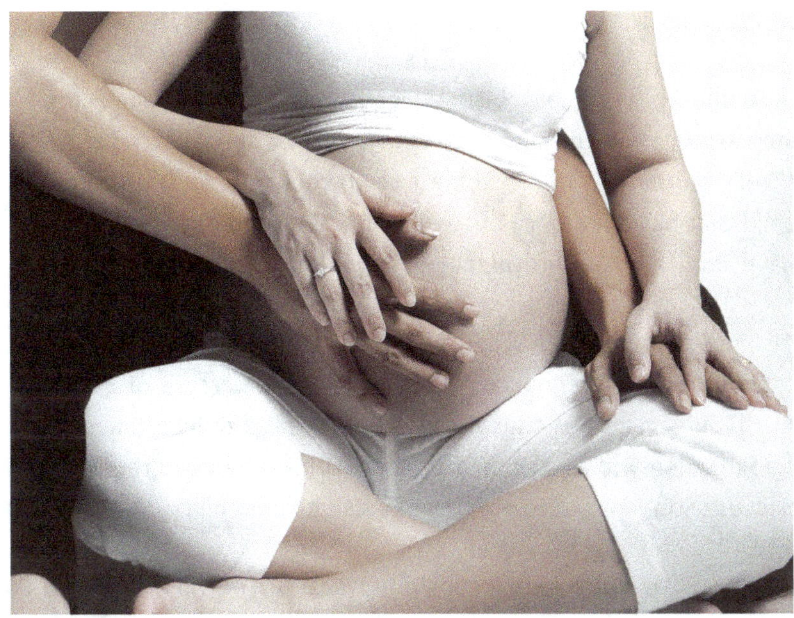

The genetic contributors and research evidence suggests that ADHD is a trait that is high hereditary in nature. Authors of studies found that 18-percent of biological parents of ADHD youths had ADHD compared to 6-percent of adoptive parents, so that means that there is a 12-percent biological connection; that's what they were finding.

Biology is an extremely high contributor to a child having ADHD and there have been other studies where they've reviewed molecular genetics and they found that ADHD comprises several disorders having different genetic and non-genetic etiologies rather than a single unitary disorder, so if somebody has been diagnosed with ADHD genetically that they may not only have ADHD but they may have other things linked to that but that this is getting like very specific in etiology.

They have also found out that the co-morbidity of ADHD meaning that if you have ADHD you are likely to have a bipolar disorder a conduct disorder or oppositional defiant disorder.

In addition, very low birth-weight children have been found increased prevalence of inattentive ADHD and the hyperactive ADHD and so that's something else to recognize that if there is a child that has been born of two pounds or three pounds, they may have a much higher prevalence of developing ADHD.

Also 22-percent of ADHD children had a maternal history of smoking during pregnancy as compared to 8-percent of the non-ADHD subjects, so of course we've heard this a million times don't smoke when you're pregnant or don't drink when you're pregnant because you may have negative effects on your child.

So and there's also family contributors to ADHD; boys with ADHD are more likely to have mothers with a major depressive episode or marked anxiety symptom and within the past year and fathers with a childhood history of ADHD, that just also contributes to the idea that you do need to look at the genetic history of a family in order to make a good diagnosis.

They may have oppositional defiance disorder or conduct disorder or they may have fathers who have had that; all of these things are overlapping as far as a diagnosis. And also there have been found some possible neuro-developmental factors cognitive and neuro neurological contributors that may contribute to the development of ADHD; so but at this point there's no single profile of ADHD.

CHAPTER 7- PARENT'S ROLE ON THEIR ADHD CHILD

With the diagnosis of your child with Attention Deficit Disorder, you may feel a shower of emotions: remorse, a feeling of not being in charge, or comfort for now being aware of your child's problem, or frustration.

However in the midst of all this turmoil, do not forget that your child's situation is not out of control. There are a number of ways in which you can help your child use his talents, and deal with ADD.

The first most important step is to properly do your research and know everything about ADD. You would thus be in a better position to help your child, and understand the problems.

You would also become more aware of the popular treatments, and be more prepared to face what might come next. It should also be helpful in preparing you to work with the doctor for managing the disorder successfully.

ADHD and Autism
With the advice of your doctor, you should also plan whether you should get your child medicated. This depends on your individual opinion and the decision is entirely personal.

According to some parents, being able to provide their children with means to lead a normal life is the best opportunity that they can give. But, for others, medication is not a good choice. However, no matter what you decide, you should be sure of it and well informed about your choice.

In any case, even if you are using medication, some strategies of behavior therapies should be applied to help manage your child's actions. These prepare your child with lasting skills to provide them with help in becoming efficient and productive.

The strategies for your child's actions and the consequences should be set by you. Children suffering from ADD need to have well defined limits set on their actions and must be treated with steady discipline.

You should be your child's best supporter, and must encourage your child. Make sure that the way they are treated at school and at home, in such that it would guarantee you child's progress. You, along with the teachers and doctors, should be like a team whose target must be to assist your child in being successful.

So lend a hand and help your child grow to be a self-assured and joyful person. Recognize their potential and let them know to what extent you love them. A child diagnosed with ADD habitually goes through depression and low sense of worth.

So if you see such cases arising then take necessary actions to steer clear of this outcome. And if the situation demands, request for expert help.

Joining a good support group and reaching out to people who share the same state of affairs, could be useful. Often the top suggestions you can get is from a person who has been through a similar situation. Make use of the experiences of life!

Chapter 8- Know More about Autism and Its Contributors

You may have seen an autistic child or adult and never knew that the person had a diagnosis. Your ignorance about the disorder is not uncommon because most people who are not experienced with the disorder look at autistic people as those who are mentally retarded or have some learning disability. This is not true. Autism is a very complicated disorder that affects children typically from the age of three to conception. The disorder is neurological in nature and primarily affects the areas of the brain where communication and social interaction is developed. To the unsuspecting person, the autistic child or adult would be considered mentally unstable or retarded.

The unique thing about autism and the reason it is sometimes hard to detect is that the disorder affects different sufferers in different levels of complexity. A mildly affected child may be able to communicate their wants and needs, but there communication is often stifled and they do not understand the subtleties of the

English language. Sometimes humor, irony, and other nuances of the language will present a difficult or impassible barrier to the child's communication process. Another autistic sufferer may have severe autism where the child or the adult cannot communicate at all. The sad thing is that the autistic person can think about the what they want to say and how to communicate it, but the words do not come out and their silence on appears on the outside.

Can you imagine trying to communicate with your teacher or parent and the words won't come out? You know the answer to the question and you know how to do the task, but the communication and the rest of your body just doesn't come out. That is why it is difficult for both teachers and parents to understand what autism is and how to deal with it. The child cannot even communicate its wants and needs during play with other children. A simple act of digging with a sand shovel can be an awkward movement or grunt that would be totally misunderstood by the other child.

Autistic children act differently to normal situations than other kids. Loud noises, a deviation from a familiar route, or a change in time schedule can set an autistic child off with sometimes violent consequences. The acts of an autistic child could be misinterpreted as a behavior disorder or an emotional disorder. Simple communication is not there. If a autistic child is hot, it has been reported that some will strip naked in public and run around. The communication is there. They are hot. It is cooler when I am naked. Therefore I will be naked and be cool. Again, the communication is there, but the socially accepted communication in which we communicate is not.

According to statistics, almost four million children will be born with autism in the next decade. The diagnoses of autistic children are becoming more refined, but think about the number of children misdiagnosed in the past where there learning and life skill accommodations were not met by professionals. Autism is a tragic disorder and many parents should be given kudos for the extra time and energy it takes to raise an autistic child. In this e-book you will learn the characteristics of autism, its symptoms, treatments, and learning strategies that will help both you and your child. Though the definition of autism is still sketchy for health care professionals and psychologists, you will learn more about autism and have a more definitive approach when dealing with autism as a teacher, parent, or someone who works with these special people.

Contributors to Autism

Autism is a mystery for most health care professionals. They have found no one clear cause for autism though there are several factors that are common throughout the research. The most common is that autistic sufferers have abnormalities in their brain. When compared to non-autistic people, autistic brains are shaped differently and function differently. There are many theories concerning the factors that contribute to autism in which genetics, heredity, and environmental aspects are suspected. The genetic theory is supported that in some families there are patterns of disabilities and mental illness that are frequent and autism is considered apart of this pattern.

What causes the mutations or the passing of the autistic gene is uncertain. Some researchers believe that a group of unstable genes interfere with the development of the brain during the early years of life and these genes rearrange themselves to hinder the proper realignment of brain tissue. If this is truly a factor for the contribution to autism then it cannot be stopped with today's medical knowledge. If the genes are isolated, genetic screening before pregnancy can determine if the parents have a predisposition to give birth to an autistic child.

Environmental factors have been another theory that researchers have come up with. The research for this idea is very sketchy and according to the Agency for Toxic Substances and Disease Registry there has been no link between autism and an outside source such as chemicals or other toxins in the environment. Remember that this may be a link and the research is just not showing the connection yet. With all the pollution that is in our air and water and all the contaminants we consume in our food, there is all likelihood that environmental factors are indeed a piece in the puzzle.

Physical medical condition has shown a possibly of being a contributing factor.

Conditions such as tuberous sclerosis and congenital rubella syndrome has yielded results that there is a high percentage of autistic manifestations after diagnosis. Also phenylketonuria also known as PKU and fragile X syndrome has been known to contribute a high number of cases that also link themselves to autism. The jury is still out to whether these conditions have percentages high enough to officially correlate evidence that leads to autism, but at this point the suspicion is there.

The contributing factors are sketchy at best, but there are factors that you can rule out. For some reason autistic kids have a predisposition to the autistic condition. You can't blame the parents for the parents have no control over their DNA. If a family does have a high occurrence of disabilities, they should still have right and the ability to procreate and to have happiness as a family. Environmental conditions are also not completely to blame unless a parent on purpose puts toxins into their bodies before or during pregnancy. Some say that drugs and alcohol consumption by the parent is a contributing factor. So far there is no link to drugs, alcohol, or alcohol fetal syndrome and autism. For now we have to accept autism for what it is.   The child, parents, or genetics are not to be blamed until there is more research done and more evidence that point to one contributing factor. For now until that research is done we must do everything we can to let the silent voices be heard and help those already inflicted with this terrible disorder.

Autism and Genetics

Right now, genetics seem the only real connection for a cause and effect in regards to autism. Genetic research is being done right now and the call for research from the National Autistic Society is desperate. They are willing to look at any research in the realm of genetics and autism and will help correlate future research with what they have in their archives now. There are some promising breakthroughs but there is not enough evidence to support a grounded theory. The only general theme that has been found is that there is a genetic link between close relatives and the sufferers of autism.

The search for the specific gene that causes this link is not under study. The Collaborative Autism Project and the International Genetic Study have been studying chromosomes that might have an influence on whether a child is autistic or not. This sounds difficult, but researchers are not even sure that it is just one gene that causes autism. If more than one gene affects autism outcomes, then even though the chance of finding one of those genes is statistically greater, the excitement and following research may ignore the others. Both research facilities have come to one conclusion but it is a weak one at best. They believe that the gene might be found in chromosome 7 of our genetic makeup. This means they have found a possible haystack and now they have to look for the needle.

Dr. Michael Dougherty of the American Institute of Biological Sciences argues the pure genetic cause theory. He thinks that there is a combination between both genetics and environmental factors. This could be true because outside environmental changes affect both phenotypical and genotypical characteristics of an organism. He believes that chromosome 12 is the main culprit to the genetic side of autism. If a child receives two mutated copies of this chromosome the amino acids that are a part of food proteins cannot be broken down. This would lead to a mutation in the development of the brain and particularly the part of the brain that controls communication and social skills. He adds that the presence of phenylketonuria may call another malfunction of the brain that produces behavior that will be diagnosed as autism. Since the PKU can be detected at birth and when detected, a special diet thwarts the negative side effects; both PKU and genetics have duel roles in the creation of autism.

The collaboration to find data and share research on autism is still in its infancy. The collaboration process between researchers only began in 1996. This means only a decade has been dedicated to finding the source of the disorder. The gene mapping projects that have fascinated researchers for years have yielded results to the cause and some cures of many diseases since it has begun. This give hopes to people who have autistic children and also hope to prospective parents who think that might be predisposed to the gene. Remember though, if the gene is found it is only a step to the cure. The gene's discovery will only allow the medical community to let parents know they have a predisposition before pregnancy and once pregnant the disorder has a good chance of occurring. Only time and patience will be needed to find both the cause and the cure of this disturbing disorder. All the parents can do for their child that has the disorder is to love them and give them the quality of life that they deserve. As with all diseases, autism will someday be a thing of the past.

CHAPTER 9- SYMPTOMS OF AUTISM AND MORE

The symptoms of autism are hard to define because each autistic child is unique in their own way. Not only are the symptoms individualized but the severity of the disorder also differs from child to child. One child might have mild autism and be able to function normally at home or in the classroom. The only difference you might see is minor social awkwardness when interacting with other or a certain preference of where there food is positioned on a plate. On the severe side you might see a child that has no communication skills. They are impulsive and their behavior, though no fault of theirs, borders on one that is socially unacceptable. Some autistic children have no fear of social norms.

One of the symptoms of autism is a delayed or unusual speech pattern. When young severe autistic children will grunt, stutter, or talk slowly with long breaks between each word or syllable. Mild autistic children have been known to memorize entire books or scripts from a television show. There was a case in Maine where a teenage autistic boy could not tell you what he had for breakfast or what his mother's name was but he could tell you, by cabin, the entire passenger manifest of the Titanic.

Other cases have included numbers in their speech pattern. A autistic child in Texas had the unusual talent of counting the number of letters of each word as you spoke them. The count was accurate and immediate, but again, simple knowledge was almost impossible to communicate.

Subtle nuances in language are also a symptom of autism. For example, the autistic child would not understand humor or would find humor in something that was not funny. The emotional reaction to irony or sarcasm would seem out of place and unusual in normal conversation. Physical comedy may be understood by the autistic child, but there actions in both body language and spoken word would seem inappropriate to the situation. When talking to an autistic child, the lack of eye contact is normally seen. They may be listening to you, but their body and eyes are concentrated on something else. You may have their full attention, but you would think that the child was totally consumed by another person or an object that has little significance to you.

The autistic child sometime does not have the ability to imagine anything outside of self. If you asked an autistic child if they would like to do what their friend is doing or how would you feel if that happened to you, they could not put the concept together to compare themselves to the other person or situation. Putting themselves in another's shoes is not a concept they can grasp or communicate. When they do communicate it may seem awkward and inappropriate. They may speak with a very high voice that seems out of place or with a very flat voice that is sometimes inaudible or hard to understand. The conversation, if they are capable will be void of any slang words or words associated in the vocabulary of a person that age.

All these nuances and symptoms of the disorder can be viewed, especially by peers, as being socially unacceptable and divergent of societal norms. Even when playing with others, the other children will have a hard time interacting with the autistic child. This could lead to isolation and further social development unless the interaction is facilitated by an understanding adult.

Speech and Communication Problems of Autism

Autism affects the speech and communication to some degree of all autistic people. The communication varies and is usually contributed to the actual mental of the brain to translate the communication and what social development the child has had. If parents of an autistic child learn and practice methods that encourage the full use of the communication skills that the child has, then the child will develop faster to meet their mental ability. Some autistic children will never gain a voice. Some are silent and rarely utter a sound while others know a few words or use grunts and noises in their effort to communicate.

On the opposite end of the autistic spectrum an autistic child may have a very rich vocabulary and are able to discuss some subjects in depth and with a great deal of intellectual insight. Others will be able to only discuss specialized subjects that either they have a great interest in or they have mastered the ability to communicate about that subject. No matter what the severity of autism is, it is not the words that they have trouble with. Most autistic children can pronounce words correctly but it how the language is used to make a coherent thought.

ADHD and Autism
The language that you hear coming out of an autistic child's mouth may be incoherent to you. The rhythm of the words or the order of the words might be totally mixed up. As the listener you would assume that the child didn't know what they were saying, but in the child's mind the message is clear; there is just a short between the brain and how the words come out of the mouth. If a child asks for a glass of water, he or she may have the sentence formed in their head, but a grunt or dislocated words will come out of their mouth.

The autistic child may repeat a phrase that they have learned to associate with a physical action. The child may have heard, "Do you want a peanut butter and jelly sandwich," from his mother and will then associate that phrase every time they are hungry. Instead of saying 'I am hungry' the child will used the same associated phrase, 'Do you want a peanut butter and jelly sandwich?' They may even use this phrase for multiple purposes. It may be used when they have to use the bathroom or they are thirsty. The language can be learned by a caring parent but all to often the child becomes frustrated when adults or peers do not understand them.

Other trait of language in the autistic child is the use of key phrases or key sounds. For example an autistic child was witnessed starting every sentence with the words, 'I like fruitcake.' No matter what he wanted or what he was trying to say, he would start the conversation with 'I like fruitcake, what is your name. I like fruitcake, where do you live?' This seems humorous at first but the child needed the phrase that he knew to facilitate the other message he was adding to it. Other autistic children will spell out a word they know like their name. For example they will say, 'M-I-K-E, that spells Mike, what is your name. That one bit of ingrained information that seems disjointed is all they need to pull out the complete thought that follows. Remember when dealing or communicating with an autistic child, have an open mind to what they are communicating. Their words can or can not be taken literally and their meaning may be the total opposite of what you are thinking.

Autism and Body Language

Now that we have learned that autism creates havoc with verbal speech and the communication between the brain and how speech is produced, we now have to look at how autism affects body language. Body language is the second form of communication that humans use to express their wants and emotions. As with speech, the autistic child has difficulty or no skill at all deciphering what a person is saying with facial expressions or body language. If you want someone to come closer you wave to them. If you want somebody to know your angry, you usually have a scowl on your face. If you are sad or happy, you can see the emotion in your facial expression and how you move your body.

The autistic child does not have an understanding or either body language of facial expression. They are in a world that is centered in themselves and the nuances of a gesture or hand motion is lost to them. Most autistic children have a hard time making eye contact during conversation. If the adult speaking or working with them does have this knowledge of no eye contact, it can be very for that adult to understand what is happening. It can be frustrating for both the adult and the child when that simple knowledge can save a lot of grief. The child may be listening to you and maybe even understand what you have said, but there attention and focus looks like it is on something else.

The autistic child may not even be looking at what you are thinking they are looking at. Eye contact is a simple human reaction to communication and that reaction within them does not exist. Even the simple activity of pointing to something you want can be lost in translation to the untrained parent or teacher. If the child is pointing at a cookie, the cookie may not be the object of his or her desire. The cookie is a symbol that may represent that they are hungry or it may be so abstract that the shape of the cookie, round, is the same shape as the toilet and they need to use the restroom. Even color may be an indication of a connection between a want and an abstract idea. It takes time and observation and a lot of out of the box thinking to link the communication patterns of an autistic individual.

The autistic child will have trouble associating your voice and your words in exactly what you want from them. Even their name may not be recognizable to them in their brain and the response to your words may be slow or may not be attended to at all. For this reason some autistic children who have not been diagnosed yet will have a diagnosis of a hearing problem. This is not the case. The child just does not know to respond to your words and if they respond it may not be in the manner that the parent or other adult expects.

The use of grammar in a sentence for mild autistic child is again a problem.

Personal pronouns and verb agreement sometimes do not meet what the adult wants the child to say. You may say, 'it is your birthday today,' and the child will repeat the entire sentence back to you without changing the your to my. First, second, and third person is not always used correctly or will not be used at all. Some autistic children will be stuck on one view of person and will use it in every context. It takes patience and time to be able to build a communication process, and even with both the autistic child may never be able to communicate their needs.

CHAPTER 10- COMMON CAUSES OF AUTISM

Thought some research disclaim that autism can spring from the use of vaccines, doctors belonging to the American Academy of Pediatrics have found enough concern that they issues a statement about nine years ago that goes against that research. The statement of concern was about thimerosal, a preservative that is used in vaccines and, believe it or not, contains mercury. Research has proved that mercury is very toxic and can cause neurological and motor functions to misfire creating some pretty dramatic disorders in children and adults.

Not only doe's mercury cause motor and neurological disorders, it can also affect the immune system and cause behavior dysfunctions. So what happens if you or your child is vaccinated with a vaccine that contains thimerosal? Could a little of each disorder come into the child and affect him or her in such a way that autism is diagnosed. Look at the symptoms of autism and then look at the multiple disabilities and disorders mercury can cause.

ADHD and Autism
This might explain the range of disabilities from mild to severe in an autistic child.

Even the Food and Drug Administration stated that some infants, depending on how much thimerosal was in the vaccine and how long between each vaccine, may be exposed to high levels of ethyl mercury. This difference in dosage and time between dosages is another clue to the severity or mildness that autistic children suffer. It only makes since that if a child has had a large dosage of ethyl mercury and has those dosages close together, especially in the early development of the body and brain, than that child would have more severity in their autism symptoms than a child who had less mercury administered to them.

If you compare the symptoms of mercury poisoned children with the symptoms of autistic children, the similarities are amazingly close. So what comes first, the mercury or the autism? The statistics alone are enough to warrant caution just because they state that autism has been counted to have alarming increases since the early 1990s.

As the vaccines given to infants to prevent hepatitis B and HIB in children increased last decade, so have the incidents of children being diagnosed with autism. Not only is this curious, but the correlation of vaccines to autism is almost exponential.

This seems like enough evidence to warrant an investigation into the link of mercury preservatives in vaccines and the amazing amount of autistic and mercury poisoned children that have been diagnosed. Parents of vaccinated children are seeing their once intelligent, bright, and socially normal child turn into a child that is wrought with fevers, night terrors, and severe behavior disorders that can be closely associated to some behaviors associated with autistic children. Even polio and chicken pox vaccines are suspect at causing autistic type symptoms and parents and doctors are beginning to question the practice.

The manufactures of mercury based vaccines have refused to provide research about the link between mercury and autism and have declined to prove any evidence that correlation does not exist. If you have an autistic child, look at their vaccination records. If you see a vaccine that might contain ethyl mercury, contact the Center for Disease Control to spur government agencies to fund more research.

Autistic Mice

About ninety out of every ten thousand person born in the United States will have a diagnosis of autism before they are three years old. Boys will have a significantly higher chance of contracting these horrible disorders than will girls. The causes of autism have not been determined as of yet, but researchers at the University of Texas are coming closer than most have yet. They have found the traits of autism such as poor social interaction and high sensitivity in mice. The researchers believe if they can find the cause of the behaviors exhibited in the mice, they will be one step closer to finding the cause of human autism.

What the researchers can do with mice, they cannot do with human subjects. They intend to examine the brain of this autistic mice and specifically the area of the brain that deals with learning and memory. Though autism affects the ability to communicate and interact with people around you, the researchers feel that the chemical reactions in the brains of the mice will be similar to those who experience autism. Proper communication is a learned behavior and your brain area that has the job of producing memory and learning is supposed to allow you to accept this information.

ADHD and Autism
Without the proper neurons or the interaction of chemicals in your brain, the communication process will be lost.

The researchers are focusing of the Pten gene because this gene has the history of being associated with other brain disorders. The similarity of autistic traits within the mice could be associated with the similarity of autism and brain disorders found among humans. The mice studied showed that they were not as curious as other mice in the pen. When a new animal was introduced, the autistic mice showed little interest. The same goes with an autistic child. When a new person enters the home or the classroom, the autistic child will be uninterested while the non-autistic children will show great interest and even try to communicate with the new comer.

The mice would not build nests nor would they look after their babies. They would show disinterest in any of the normal goings on of normal mice. The mice seemed disinterested in anything except their primal needs of food, water, and defecation. When exposed to stimuli such as a loud noise or sudden movement like being picked up, the autistic mice would act like an autistic child by overreacting to the stimuli. The mice would scream and refrain from physical stimuli just as most autistic children run from or cover their ears when over stimulated.

The only behaviors that were not in correlation between the mice and human autistics were the repetitive behaviors or the obsessive motions that most human autistic children exhibit. The only other similarities were that the mice had a larger head and larger brain volume that is traditionally a symptom of human autism. Researchers believe that if they can find the gene responsible for the autistic like behaviors in the mice the quest to find the cause and cure of autism may be one step closer. This research proves that there is hope for a autistic sufferers and if not for them, then for the thousands of autistic children that are yet to be born.

CHAPTER 11- MORE RESEARCH ON AUTISM

Autism has increase 172% in the 1990s. Why? This disorder that impairs language and impedes social skills is becoming a rising phenomena that is affecting thousands of children, mainly males, in the United States and the world. The autistic child is characterized by repetitive movements, obsessive desires, lack of eye contact, and socially impaired or unacceptable behavior. Even though the autistic child may not show these signs at birth, the symptoms will appear at about the age of a year and a half, and the child will slowly loose what speech or communication they had gained previously.

To this date there is no cause or cure that can be determined. Though research has speculated of genetic disorders or vaccine related incidents, there is no concrete evidence that autism derives from any of these theories. There has been foundations set up in the Colorado area that are beginning to gather data about autism. The start was slow and the patience of parents with autistic children is wearing thin. The physical and mental exhaustion of raising an autistic child is beginning to show on parents, teachers, and medical personal.

The parents of these children are spending thousands in special classes that deal with speech, social skills, and behavior and there money is not returning the yield of research that is needed to help this epidemic problem. Parents have spent hours scanning the web hoping for a glimmer of hope from a researcher or parent that has observed a breakthrough. The education and treatment of autistic children has reached monumental records while the government has not put in a full effort of research money into the coffer.

In the early 1990s only a dozen or so doctors or scientists were totally devoted to the study of autism. Society is just seeing the need for more research but the parents of autistic children have seen and have desired the need for almost two decades. It is estimated that the care for an autistic child will reach around four million dollars per child during their lifetime. This includes the special educational services that are draining the funds from our public schools. An autistic child who attends public school has a full time teacher, a single paraprofessional assigned to them, speech therapist, occupational therapists, behavior specialist, and psychologists.

The annual government money spent on a special education child is six thousand five hundred dollars. The money spent on the autistic child by the school system sometimes cost in excess of ten thousand dollars. The money is pulled from regular education classes, after school programs, and other programs that are vital for a public school to educate its entire population. The money comes from your taxes, but the government is doing little to facilitate research that could bring down public cost.

This is only the public's contribution indirect from the government. Think about the costs of the parents and the restriction of a right to live a normal life. These parents and teachers should be applauded, but the call for more money for research from the government has to be made. If you feel strongly about this, contact your state congressman or representative and tell them. The public and private cost of autism will rise as fast as the percentage of cases diagnosed. At a 172% increase, how the parents or we as a nation afford not to fund research.

Treatment of Autism

There have been stories and tales of a cure or magical treatment for autism. These claims are not true. They set up the hopes and dreams of both parents and teachers alike only to be disenchanted with the discovery that the claim is false. There has only been one proven treatment for autism and the treatment is not a cure. The treatment is an educational program that individually fits the autistic child's abilities and works around the disabilities to teach the child alternative forms of communication and behavioral skills which will allow them some semblance of a normal adulthood.

When an autistic child reaches school age, there will be a meeting of professionals including a psychologist, doctors, parents, speech therapists, and other interested parties who will draw up an individualize education program for the child.

The program will look at the abilities of the child and what level of achievement the child has had in the parent's home and outside services. Mainstreaming the child into regular classrooms is the goal of the program, but the child will be pulled out of mainstream classes in order to provide special services which may include a speech instructor or an behavior specialist who works on both the communication process and the behavior associated with autism.

ADHD and Autism
There are advocates that autistic children should be brought out of the mainstream classes and put into a more restrictive environment that will limit the sensory items that might distract or upset the child. The autistic child needs to have a pattern in their lives and in the mainstream classroom; the hustle and bustle of public education settings may lead them to sensory overload. Not only that but the social aspect of being different and not being able to contribute or communicate to the rest of the class can be heartbreaking to both the student and the teachers involved. The self- contained class room will break down tasks into manageable chunks that the child can be successful and maybe eventually learn.

The treatment process goes on both at home and at school. The autistic child must be taught how to appropriately interact with others. A common behavior in autistic children is to take off their clothes. They see no sense of wrong or right by being nude in public. Such behaviors need time and patience to mend and some methods might work for one child and then be completely a failure for others. Parents, teachers, and medical professionals need to keep abreast of new treatments so that they can replace a treatment or method that has been proven a failure for a particular child. Sometimes the behavior cannot be changed at all and the individualize education program must come up with strategies to deal with the behavior.

Parents and teachers must remember that the autism is a life long condition and as the child moves through life the treatments must change to fit the life period of that child. For example, when puberty come along the autistic child will discover themselves sexually and masturbation usually follows. The program must change to fit the new behavior of masturbation and in a few years it must change again to teach the child the appropriate behaviors with the opposite sex. The changes are not understood by the child, but like Pavlov's dog, a conditioned response may be instilled in the child and the proper behavior may be a learned response.

CHAPTER 12- HOW TO DIAGNOSE AUTISM

Autism diagnoses are different than most diagnoses of other disorders. It may take doctors years to finally gather up enough evidence for the diagnoses of autism. Parents usually are suspect long before the diagnoses is given because they can see that the child may not give them eye contact or that the communication process that the child has learned has started to regress after the first year and a half or so of life. The average age for diagnoses in this country is between the age of two and three and that is where the symptoms start to manifest themselves.

The difficulty in the diagnosis of autism is mainly due to the developmental changes a child goes through during the first three years of life. When a child is developing quickly the nuances of communication and social behavior may elude doctors or even parents who are not specifically watching their child for autism. The pattern of a child's development is ever changing and without a close eye and experience, the onslaught of autism is almost impossible to catch. Even the slightest social blunder may be that the child just has some odd quirks and the line between these quirks and minor autism is a very thin one.

Only the judgment of the doctor is the determining factor to label a child autistic. Some autistic children have gone through their entire life with the label of emotionally disabled or behaviorally challenged. Many doctors stay away from this label because of the emotional impact on the parents or care providers and the chance of lawsuits if the label causes adverse reactions later in life. There are no medical tests that can be administered that would clearly define autism. The doctor's opinion is the only thing that will label a child and put them in a category among special needs that hasn't even really been defined or researched much.

The criterion for autism is determined by a panel of doctors who compare related cases and find a common symptom. Though the criterion is sketchy at best, right now it is the only way some doctors can comfortably make a diagnosis. Most clinicians and medical personal use the Diagnostic and Statistical Manual for Mental Disorders to classify autism and the basic guidelines only include the manifestations of communication use and social behavior. Another guideline that is usually diagnosed as compulsive behavior is the constant vigilance toward established patterns or norms.

The autistic child will find their comfort zone in a specific path they will walk around their house or at school. They may be schedule oriented in which they will follow a specific schedule and will refuse to deviate from it. If a autistic child is made to change their pattern they will lose control of emotions and behavior. Behavior exhibited could be uncontrolled anger to verbal confrontation of an unpleasant manner. The need to follow the specific pattern in built into their system as a way to deal with an ever changing world.

The one thing that the criterion does not cover is the fixation on certain things.

Some autistic children can memorize entire books if it is something that they really like. One autistic boy in Wyoming could recite the entire series of Dr. Seuss books. He would recite the entire book including the title and reference sections.

Myths Surrounding Autism

As with all disorders that people do not understand, myths and claims are made out of ignorance and become apart of urban legend that confuses the public and puts misinformation out there that could detrimental to the parent looking for an answer to their dilemma. Autism is a disease with an unknown cause and an unknown cure. This mysterious mental disorder is something for parents to be frightened about and the myths that pop up on the internet or in conversation does not help the placate the emotions of the parent who is facing life with an autistic child.

One of the myths of autism is that autism is caused by an uncaring or distant parent. This is an awful presumption that should be stifled when ever heard. Autism is a neurological brain disorder that makes the child have anti-social or poor social habits.

The environment or relationship between mother and child has nothing to do with the cause of the disease. The relationship with a distant mother may only the hinder the timeliness of a diagnosis because she was not paying attention to the symptoms, but the assumption that the relationship is the cause of the disease is false.

Another myth that has circulated is that autistic children and idiot savants are the same thing. Amazing feats of memorization or counting has been seen in very few autistic children. Most autistic children fixate on a subject or a genre and become experts in it, but others have no abilities at all. The fixation may be root of the myth and the very few that exhibit these incredible mental powers are often exploited and have been shown to wide audiences. The Tom Cruise movie 'Rain Man' centered on a autistic adult with counting prowess and this could be where the public passes on this myth.

A myth brought on by marketers and promoters of nutritional supplements is the idea that special diets and nutritional supplements can cure autism. This may be great if you are a parent that is desperately searching for something that will help their kid, but the only thing a special diet or nutritional supplement will do for the child is to make them a healthier autistic child. The autism will still be there, but as with every human, the nutritional supplements and diet will only make the autistic child healthy and not cure the neurological imbalance the exists.

Another sad myth is that children with autism will never have the comfort of human relationships. This is completely false. Autistic children just communicate differently than others. They may feel love and hate but they cannot display the emotion as the rest of society would expect it to be shared. Autistic adults have fell in love, gotten married and even have had a series of successful relationships as single adults. Autistic couples are common with high functioning autism and they more than any one else understands the pain of not being able to communicate the emotion they are feeling.

If you hear somebody spreading these myths around, confront them and set them straight. These kinds of myths dismantle what parents, teachers, and medical professionals have been trying to build for years and that is a true understanding of autism. Such falsehoods can shake the resolve of parents who have autistic children and destroy hopes of finding the cause and a cure. The parents are desperate to find both and these myths only dump on their dreams.

Chapter 13- Symptoms of Autism in Infants

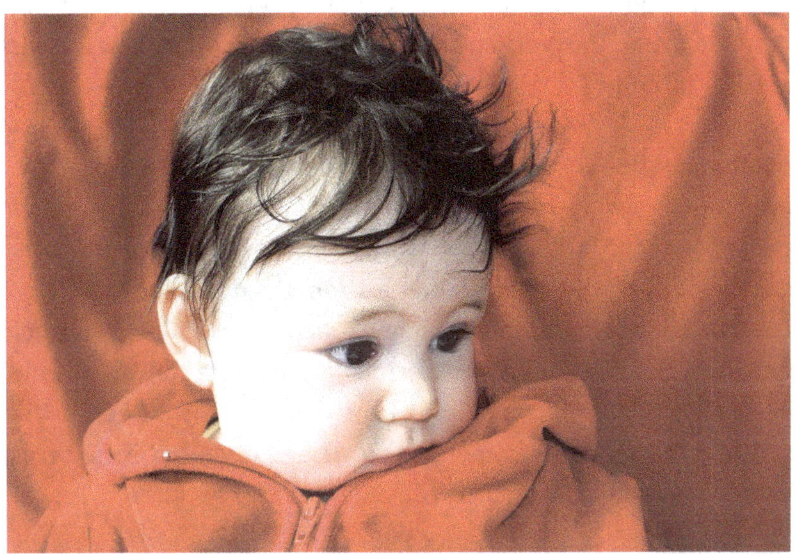

With the incidents of autism up 172% since the 1990s, parents are anxious to find out if their baby has a chance to acquire autism. Seven out of every ten thousand infants will develop autism within the first three years of life. The sad thing about the diagnosis of autism is that the symptoms are subtle to about one and half years of age and most doctors and even parents are hard pressed to find what symptoms they should worry about and what symptoms they should ignore. Since the baby is developing so fast, the symptoms do not usually manifest themselves until you see the baby regressing from the speech and social skills they have learned so far.

Remember that not one single behavior will point to autism, though a single symptom should not be ignored. The diagnosis of autism is still largely undefined because the autistic child can acquire various degrees of the disorder. The first thing a parent should be aware of is loss of some speech or behavior that has been learned and is now not demonstrated. For example is the words Daddy or Mommy was in the vocabulary and for some reason they are used less and less, the child may be loosing the brain function for memory and communication. If the words are dropped from the vocabulary all together and no new words replace, it is time for concern.

Another subtle symptom that could or could not be autism is the formation of two sentence words by the second year of age. If a child cannot for simple sentences like 'Daddy go' or 'Mommy love' it come be that your child is suffering from the onslaught of autism. This is not always the case though. Your child may have another disability that deals with speech and language or a learning disability and autism should not be considered the object of the speech process, but is something to look at if you have concerns that your infant has the ability to obtain autism.

At an even younger age, around the first year, if your child does not say any words or even babble, then your concerns might be warranted for autism. Remember there are other disorders out there that manifest themselves in the same way, but the autistic aware parent should count this as one of the major symptoms and should be concerned. If your child displays one or any of these characteristics, than you should take them to a medical professional. Remember from the previous chapters that doctors who are unfamiliar with autism will be hesitant to diagnose the disorder. If you are not happy with the diagnoses of your doctor, take your child to a few more so you will have a clear conscious and a satisfied mind.

Another thing is to watch your baby's body language and expression of emotion.

If you are warm and cuddly with your baby and your baby does not react the way you have seen other babies, this could be a red flag for autism. Observe other reactions such as severe stress over loud noises or sudden moves. If you are talking to your baby and you get no response or you wave your hands in front of your baby and there is no eye contact or reaction, there is probably something wrong. Even if it is just a feeling that you have, you need to seek medical attention so you can find out if your baby has autism or another disorder. There is no cure for autism, but an early diagnosis can not only add to the base of knowledge about autism but at the same time can help get your baby treatment as soon as possible. An early detection can also set the parents up with consoling that they need to learn how to raise an autistic child.

How Can Families Cope With an Autistic Child and the Financial Burden

If your child has just been diagnosed with autism, you and your family are about the have a life changing experience. After you get over the shock of an autistic diagnosis you and your spouse will probably be overwhelmed with all the information and misinformation there is about the disorder. Your doctor will probably suggest a team of specialists who will take on the child's case that will probably change during the child's lifetime as new symptoms appear or the child's age and needs change. The cost of an autistic child for services and care can run close to $4,000,000 during the child's lifetime and can drain savings accounts and put the family in heavy debt.

The first thing the family needs to change is their opinion of insurance. Some people will take a good job without insurance just for a good paycheck or other benefits. This can't happen anymore. The parents or a least one of the parents has to have good insurance from their employers. Without insurance your child will not get the level of care that will give them the quality of life that your child deserves. The medical costs and the supplemental costs of going to different therapists and clinicians can put your bank account in financial shock and without insurance there will be little room for recovery.

Another thing to worry about is that you will get little financial assistance from the government. The Americans with Disabilities Act allows your child social security benefits and welfare, but most people who receive these funds can barely scratch out a living with today's economy. The supplemental money will have to come from the parent's wages and whatever other financial options there are. In some cases there are clinical trials or case studies that will pay for the treatment for your child, but these are usually experimental and if your child is in the control group of the experiment, then any benefits will be negated. The control group is the group where nothing new is done to them or a placebo is given instead of medication. A clinical trial can help with the finances but could be heartbreaking for the family if not benefit is seen.

If you have the finances and the opportunity you might want to consider moving outside of the United States. European countries and Canada have a different philosophy in financing families with children with autism than does the United States. The United States will spend millions in the public school system to have your child taken care of educationally through special education programs. Since autism is a unique disorder that is individualized most teachers, though they are trained, will not have the same relationship with the child as the parents. European countries and Canada siphon their monies in a different way. Instead of paying the doctors and teachers, they pay the parents and let them choose the method of treatment and the path of education. This will let the money go directly to the family and not a school system that is poorly suited to devote this cash to the development and the treatment of the child. Most of the time in public schools, autistic children are put with the mentally retarded and severely disabled children who have totally different issues and learning styles. If moving out of the country is not an option for you, you might want to find a financial advisor that will help you plan for the future and the future expenses of your autistic child. Stay insured and do not let your insurance lapse.

The Difference Between Asperger's Syndrome and Autism

According to the DSM-IV classifications asperger's syndrome and autism are two separate disorders. There is debate however because aspergers and autism exhibit some of the same symptoms. The argument is that aspergers is a form an autism and should not be listed as a separate entity when diagnosing the disorder or when devising treatment. The argument relies on the idea that since there is no distinct criteria for either disorder and they are both persuasive developmental disorders they should be treated the same.

The argument about name is not just an argument on syntax, but an argument for services and label. The services for an autistic child are far more extended than a child diagnosed with asperger's syndrome. The group that wants to keep the labels different look at the argument from a research based idea. They want to see both syndromes separate because research and treatment will follow two different paths and the benefits of one path might bleed over to the other. This way is there is a break through in asperger's syndrome, that break through may help the autistic child.

According to the DSM-IV the diagnosis for both disorders are very similar. The clinicians who diagnosis the patient looks at the severity of the symptoms and diagnose on the severity of certain symptoms and the lack of severity in others. This gives the doctor some leeway in the diagnoses but also leads to the idea that the diagnoses is not a stringent as it appears or needs to be. The DSM-IV proponents argue that there needs to be more criteria in the guidelines for both disorders in order to make a correct diagnosis

The major distinction that now can be read from the manual is that autism, a communication disorder, does not allow the child to communicate normally. This is different in an asperger's child because the asperger's child may not understand the communication that is presented to them. The autistic child understands but is not able to neither respond to the communication nor give the proper response that is socially acceptable. With an entire list of specifications for the disorder, it is sketchy that this one ill defined symptom can be the separating point.

Another sticky difference between the disorders is the patient's ability to have an average intelligence. Some autistic children are mentally retarded. Though not all, some have met the criteria that their IQ is below the measured rating of mental retardation which is 69. The asperger's child cannot be diagnosed with the disorder if they have IQ with is 69 points or lower. Most asperger's children have average to above average intelligences. This is another argument. How many children that have asperger's syndrome are diagnosed as autistic just because they have a score that labels them as mentally retarded? There is room for a lot of misdiagnosis and because of that there are a lot of children that are in the wrong treatment programs.

If you are a parent of an autistic child that has a below average IQ, you might want to look in to petitioning the diagnosis if the programs for as asperger's syndrome child is more beneficial for your child. Just because your child has the diagnosis of autism, the case can be reviewed and with time and patience, you can find a team that will make an alternative diagnoses.

Chapter 14- Dog Assistance for Autistic Patients

Your autistic child is not blind nor has a physical disability that renders them helpless, but most autistic children do lack the ability to make safe choices. Parents of autistic children are diligent, they have to be, but wouldn't be safer and give the parents more peace of mind is there was an extra set of eyes watching their child. Now there is a service that provides canine assistance to autistic sufferers. 4Paws, the first autistic assistance dog agency, has dogs that can be placed with your autistic child and with a doctor's approval no family can be turned away.

One of the most disturbing phenomena concerning autism is the child's ability to just run away. You can be washing dishes and as soon as you turn your back your child can be gone. There are normal situations in which a autistic child can make very dangerous. They can fall into a pool or run into traffic and you would hardly know they were gone. An autistic assistance dog would alert you if your autistic child was to deviate from their normal pattern. Either by barking or by gaining your attention physically, the autistic assistance dog will give you enough warning to catch the child before they put themselves into danger.

Not only will the dog alert you that the child is missing but they will help you track and find the child. The bond between the child and dog is something special and that bond will instill the dog to protect and find your lost child. This relationship tends to be odd for more autistic children because the bonding process does not happen sometimes even if it is a human relationship. The communication process sometimes even excludes the parent from a loving relationship. Testimonials from parents who have received autistic assistance dogs say that they are amazed at how the animals and children interact.

Another benefit to both parents and the child is the parent's report that the child has more feelings and compassion toward their dog then they do toward siblings or adults. The parents also state that once the dog is placed in the home, the autistic child shows less aggression and anger. In one case a parent said that there autistic child stopped showing frustration all together. Before the canine assistant the child would throw temper tantrums and physically attack the person they were angry at. Now the child, when frustrated, goes and hugs his dog until the anger goes away.

Another behavior that is trained to the assistant dog is to recognize repetitive behavior. If a child is prone to hand flapping as many autistic children demonstrate, it usually takes the touch of a parent to redirect the behavior. Now that is the dog's responsibility. The dog will gently touch or nuzzle the child when the behavior happens and the child will learn through conditioned response that they are presenting a negative behavior and the behavior will stop.

ADHD and Autism

The only reason that a dog will not be placed in your home is if your home is not suitable for the pet. The cleanliness of your home and your financial ability to own a pet is severely scrutinized. Also the safety of the pet is looked at. If your child is so violent that the dog may be injured because of a temper tantrum or other aggressive action, the agency has the right to deny you a dog or to pull the dog from your home. If you have a puppy that you would like trained to be an autism assistant dog, 4Paws does offer a school in which you, the child, and the dog will be taught to work together as a team.

Teaching Autistic Children

If you are a parent of an autistic child you need to put your child in a structured environment as soon as he or she is diagnosed. Studies have proved that a structured environment that provides nurturing and teaching is the best method to start to teach the social skills and behavior redirection that your child needs. This can be an exhausting job for a parent that leaves no time for personal relaxation or freedom of the stress it takes in raising such a child. A team effort needs to be extended from other professionals that service the child to turn taking between siblings and parents.

Your child will probably start formal public school at around the age of five or six.

Before this age, structure and instruction is critical for the child to development within their abilities. You as a parent need to structure your day as well so that you have time to deal with daily tasks and find some kind or recreation outside your child's life.

Recreation for the parents is important for the parent's mental well being as well as quality of life. First you have to come up with a plan with realistic goals. You need to know what activities your child will participate in what they will learn from it. You also need to plan

When teaching your autistic child, remember not to use a long strand of phrases. It is best to give clear concise ideas that go together. You might want to add tags to the meanings of the phrases. For example if you are teaching the difference from left to right and the words left to right. Affix a piece of paper to yours or your child's hand with words left and right on them. Most autistic children do not see in words, they see in pictures. With the paper placed on the hands, not only does the child see the movement of the hands but can associate the words left and right with it.

After awhile you will notice that your child is good at something such as drawing or building blocks. You have to be creative, but find someway of including what they are good at into the lesson you wish them to learn. Maybe you are teaching them the word me. Find a picture of your child and put the word me on it. Have the child draw a picture of themselves and to finish the drawing have them write me on the picture. This may be a repetitive process and you may have to change it up a little, but eventually the concept will be learned.

If you notice you child is fixated on something like a book, movie, or map, again put that fixation to work with you. Earlier in this e-book the story of a autistic boy's fixation with the Titanic was discussed. The teacher or parent could use characters and actions of the Titanic story to reinforce behavior, concepts, or social skills. Again you will have to be creative and this type of teaching is not the norm for most educators.

You have to think outside of the box as the child is trying to not only get the message from inside the box, but to find the box in the first place.

ADHD and Autism
If you are teaching reading do not concentrate on one form of instruction. Some autistic children can learn by phonics and some by sight words. Do not restrict your method of instruction. Try both methods to see which one is right for your child.

Research has shown that a combination of sight words and phonics can be a very successful for the non-autistic student and it might be a good start to get your child the way to reading and comprehension.

Sounds and visual distractions are other areas for concern when teaching the autistic child. Sounds such as school bells are fire alarms can hurt their ears and cause either a violent reaction or bad behavior. Record the sounds that the child should be used to and then let them playback the sounds at the volume of their choice. When they are comfortable with one sound, encourage them to increase the volume the volume until they can take the sound at the volume it will occur. Visual stimulation is also a problem for the autistic child. Place them at a desk with blinders and very little visual stimulation except for the task that they are doing. Even the flickering of fluorescent lighting can cause the mind and the eyes to wander from their intended task.

If you are trying to teach eye contact during conversation, physical activity or interaction is best. Swinging has been shown to increase eye contact. Only when the child wants to swing should the parent or teacher use this method. As the child is swinging talk to them. The motion that is fluid in front of them and their peripheral vision will be to much for them to concentrate on. The swinging motion will force the child to give you eye contact as you talk to them. This method takes a long time to work so the teacher or parent has to have patience and perseverance.

Don't just rely on sound and sight to teach your autistic child. You may want to try touch, especially if the child is older and the other two senses are not helping. If you want to teach your child numbers and he or she is not getting it. Try to make or buy some plastic numbers. Give them a plastic number and let them hear the word of the number. As they feel it, some connection might be made to the word and their association of touch along with the verbal connection might be enough for them to learn the word of a number. You can come up with many kinds of manipulatives, but if one doesn't work then change the manipulative before the child learns the wrong concept.

The chapter was started with the idea that the parent had to schedule teaching time in their child's and their schedule. It might be a good idea to hire a nanny or baby sitter particularly trained to teach a concept. It might even be for two to three hours a day. This will give you time to get your daily tasks complete and at the same time you know your child is being looked after by someone who is sensitive to their condition. A good activity that might work well for a nanny would just be playtime. She could teach concepts like taking turns, winning and losing, and following specific rules of the game. The child could have a social interaction lesson while you go to the grocery store or get your hair done.

Remember the education and the educational schedule for your child is important, but you have to have some 'me' time. Even if you have the patience of a god, anyone will be worn down by the constant attention to their child. If a child has speech therapy for an hour a day, schedule yourself a nap, a reading time, or just time to take a hot bath during that time. You have to break yourself away from being the constant care giver. Sure you can do it, but the stress and mental anguish you would suffer would not be a good thing for you or your child's education. You can't give up eighteen or more years of your life just to be a hero to your child. You know you can do it, but schedule time for yourself.

The Fixation Behavior of an Autistic Child

Fixation is a common characteristic in the behavior of an autistic child. The child may be fixated on a book, a picture, a person, maps, music, numbers, or a movie.

Whatever the fixation, the high functioning autistic child will become a resident expert on the subject. They will memorize and will be able to regurgitate in rote the exact amount of information they are fixated on. They may even to be able to read music aloud by sounding out the notes or something more simplistic, your child may be fixated by a music artist and have all their songs memorized.

Fixations can be a good thing. The old method of taking the fixation away from the child has been replaced with the idea of using the fixation to facilitate learning. If a child is fixated on a certain television cartoon, turn the sound off and let them read through close captioning what is going on. If they all the words to the program they are fixated on, they will soon begin to associate the words with actual audio sound. Not only does this placate the fixation, but it uses the fixation to stimulate learning in a new medium.

A little know fact about communication and fixation was what the autistic child looked at when they fixated. A research study that looked at video tapes of autistic children interacting during play showed that most of the time during verbal communication the child would fixate of objects instead of faces. When the child finally gave the person talking eye contact, the item of fixation was the mouth instead of the eyes. You can use this fact to be conscious of how your mouth moves when you are talking. If you get a positive reaction from a word, it may not be the word that motivates your child; it may be the position in which your mouth was in.

The eye contact problem has been addressed by research and the fixation of the mouth area mystery has been solved. Researchers say that the amygdale is responsible for creating a fear by looking in a person's eye. Can you imagine not being able to look anybody in the eye because your brain registers their eyes as a threat?

This is sad because for years teachers and parents have emphasized eye contact as a behavior change when actually they were making the students learn to deal with their terror.

Remember that fixation may be much more involved than just an over exuberant liking of one thing or another. The fixation may be a bridge between understanding and association. The fixation can be manipulated to a learning experience that not only contains the fixation information but adds everyday concepts to the fixation experience. Use all the senses when presenting something about the fixation and the concepts you want addressed. Let there be smells, visions, sound, and touch. If one sense does not make the connection then maybe the other sense will pick it up.

The fixation is not just misplaced attention to one subject. It is something that they can grasp and of course they are going to like it when they are actually communicating knowledge they are going to be successful at. Their brain has finally found a place of function and normalcy. To stifle their creative and learning experience by taking away their fixation may be a huge mistake. If the fixation is healthy and no a danger to the child, then embrace it and expand on it. The fixation and the concepts you teach in the alignment of that fixation can make your child's life easier and happier.

CHAPTER 15- HOW TO LIVE TOGETHER WITH YOUR AUTISTIC CHILD

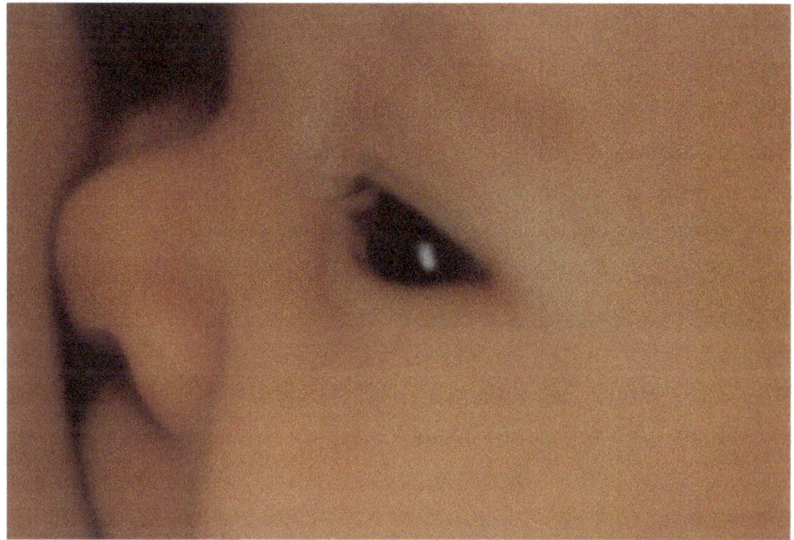

The Autism Society of America or ASA is an organization that encompasses an army of volunteers that staff a website that provides information on autism and collects donations for research and other positive autism outlets. The ASA has not only vowed to help in the education, advocacy, and treatment of autistic individuals, but they have also vowed to help the parents and the experts facilitate information of autistic issues and at the same time build a support group to help both autistic children and their families.

The ASA has continued this mission in their mission statement which declares that they will try to be the number one resource in the collection and distribution of autistic information that is presented. They intend to keep the integrity of the autistic individual intact as well as protecting the autistic community as a whole. They pledge to have a respectful communication of ideas that are positive in the needs of the autistic population and at the same time to disclaim any misinformation or myths that evolve around autism.

Stating in 1965 with a handful of parents, ASA has grown into the world's leadinr in providing information, presenting research, and providing as much reference about autism then any other source. ASA has over 200,000 members and at least 200 chapters in the United States and around the world. Not only does the ASA provide information for the teachers, parents, and individuals with autism, they also have created programs of public awareness. The more the public knows about autism, the less chance misinformation or defamatory actions will take place.

The ASA offers scholarships and rewards to students and individuals who are actively participating in the ongoing research and collection of information on autism. The scholarships may help the student or individuals pay for schooling or to continue research. There are other scholarships that deal with just funding for schooling of autistic students that need funds or who have excelled academically at a higher level of learning. Awards also go out to autism organizations of the year, parents of the year, an autistic student of the year, and the autism professional of the year. These efforts go to recognize these individuals and to encourage more participation in the autism effort.

The store at ASA doesn't have many items, only four, but if you are sincere about autism they are of great worth. They offer a support autism research rubber wristband that will tell the public about your conviction to rid the world of autism. They offer an Autism for Dummies books which breaks down the mystery of autism in layman's language. This resource can help both teachers and parents. They also offer a reference guide for autism in Spanish. Autism is not localized to any race, nationality, or religion. This guide provides information for the large Hispanic community that is present in the world. If you are really into the goings on of the ASA, the 2005 and 2006 autism conferences on audio so you can listen to the discussions live.

The site needs volunteers and supporters. Even if you are not an autistic parent, the ASA can offer you the opportunity to be apart of something greater than the individual. Sign up and participate today and maybe autism will be eradicated with your effort or donation.

Childproofing Your Home for Your Autistic Child

When you raise an autistic child, especially in the younger years, you really worry about their safety and their whereabouts. The autistic child does not react to normal stimuli nor do they respond to verbal commands as quickly as a non-autistic child. Their curiosity and lack of understanding of danger may put them in harms way more that a normal pre-school child. There are certain things you can do to make your home more autistic child friendly and these few precautions could make your household safer and give you peace of mind.

Locks and latches are the best thing to keep cabinets closed and locked from the curiosity of your autistic child. Chemicals and cleaners need to be kept locked and anytime there are in use, they need to be watched carefully. Lock away anything that could be a source of harm to your child. This could include the knife drawer, your sewing basket, chemical closets, and other things that you could foresee as a possible harm for your child. There should be locks on anything of danger especially gun cabinets and other things that would be a danger to anyone.

Using a cordless or wireless phone is a good idea as you go through the day with your autistic child. Talking on the phone and being restricted to one place during your conversation will take away your concentration on supervision. Another reason you might want to consider a cordless phone is to have the availability to call for assistance if you are your child is in danger. The wireless phone will let you tend to your business and also give you the assurance that help is just a phone call away.

It may not be the greatest danger but you should bind up your cords from your drapes and curtains. A curious mind can conjure all sorts of dangerous activities with a hanging cord. They are in danger of hanging themselves or getting caught in the cord and having a panic attack that could lead to dangerous behavior. If you have pets, an autistic child could innocently injure them by tying them to the cord. Anything that loops and could fit around the next should be put up out of reach or bound so that your child can not use it in a dangerous manner.

Not only does the inside of you house need to be childproofed, but the outside as well. Watch your child around swing sets or tire swings. Again the danger of getting caught in the chains or wrapping a rope around their neck is possible. Watch out for lawnmowers and other dangerous lawn grooming equipment. The curious mind might have watched daddy start and mow the lawn and the danger of the blades might not have stuck in the mind as much as the process of getting it started. If you have a fenced in lawn, make sure there is a latch and a lock on the gate. Autistic children have a skill of disappearing when your back is turned and it would be easier to find them in the backyard than having to search for them down the street.

This information may seem redundant, but the reality is that your child may have different motives than what you perceive. With the lack of communication skills and the lack of social behavior, the child can put themselves into a lot of danger very easily.

Just use common sense and make supervision a number one priority.

Autism and Nutritional Supplements

Autism is a terrible disorder that cripples the abilities of some parents with autistic children to reasonably discern between false hopes for cures and a research based study. Most autistic parents have searched the internet, talked to doctors, and have read scores of literature to find help in the treatment and the cure for autism. Their searches usually ends up fruitless because at this time there in no cure for autism. This is heart breaking news for the parents and sometimes it will send them down the road of the unconventional methods that promise the moon but only delivers more bills and the realization that the methods did not help.

One of the most notorious claims that are made today, that have duped millions into believing it, is that nutritional supplements can cure autism. These shysters have taken the symptoms of autism like severe gastrointestinal problems and have spun tails that just by adding nutritional supplements to the diet of the autistic child the child will regain their cognitive skills and will be able to function normally. This is not true. All you will get when giving your child nutritional supplements is a healthier autistic child.

There is no miracle cure and these companies are out for the dollar not for the cure.

The Food and Drug Administration has issued a statement that: "Parents of autistic children can be desperate and provide easy targets for unproven therapies. Marketers of dietary supplements for autistic children contend that their products promote more complete food digestion, thereby preventing neuro-toxic molecules that contribute to autism. This is a false and unsupported claim."

ADHD and Autism

To back this up there has been no founded research that backs these claims nor has any medical organization or association given even a hint of support. Even the Autistic Association of America has down played nutritional supplements as a therapy.

Educated parents in the scientific community, who have autistic children, have made a grievance with the Food and Drug Administration. They believe that the agency should not make a statement against nutritional supplements until the people who believe in them, marketers and parents alike have a say. They have asked that a forum be open to discuss home based research and they discoveries parents have made by changing the diet of their children. Without proven documented research the success of these parents cannot really be taken seriously by the scientific community. The sad thing is that if there is success, the Food and Drug Administration may be swayed by the pharmaceutical industry not to act of the information unless there is formal research.

The research that has been done on the subject is very limited. After a review of three research studies, all three seem to have a slant toward the nutritional supplement industry. The words were written in a defensive tone that pushed the supplements but gave very few actual clinical trails to the success. The data gathering method used was mostly parent surveys. There were no laboratory or scientific method guidelines that could give statistical data when correlated with a control group. Used in a qualitative model, the opinions of parents and their observations were made the focus instead of a quantitative model which would give statistics and the actual growth or retention of growth of the autistic child.

If these supplements were to work, they would alleviate some symptoms of autism but it would not be a cure. It could be easily understood why parents see improvement. If there son or daughter shows at least a notch of improvement, in their mind the treatment works.

Toilet Training the Autistic Child

Toilet training any toddler can be an adventuresome and tiring ordeal. There are many methods that have hit the markets lately and these methods can range anywhere between diapers that change color when wet to musical toilets that reward the child with music when they use the potty. This task is more difficult when your child has autism.

When communication is a problem, as with most autistic children, letting an adult know you need to use the bathroom can be almost impossible endeavor. Some autistic children reach the double digits in age before they learn to ask for and to use the toilet.

Most autistic children do not have the skill and sometimes to desire to mimic or imitate a behavior. Just because the parents are using the toilet and they demonstrate the behavior, the autistic child will refuse or not get the connection between the right or wrong of toilet training. Most autistic children's schedule is full and when you add something new to the schedule it usually upsets them emotionally. The addition of toilet training to their regiment could cause out right rebellion and bad behavior because they do not want to get outside of their normal daily activity.

If you are having trouble toilet training your autistic child, you might want to observe them for a few days before you try again. Watch and see if the child actually notices when they soil themselves. Do they reposition themselves so that they are not uncomfortable after an accident? Some autistic children feel natural in their own wastes while other will react by taking off their clothes. If your child is ignoring their soiling, consult with a doctor to see if your child has a medical condition that would prevent them from recognizing the feeling they are experiencing.

Now here is your part in toilet training. You need to relax and not stress over it. Time will make it happen and your stress and high emotion will only cause the stress of your child. Even the most conscious parent will overreact when they have to change yet another diaper. If your child sees it's no big deal for you, then they can relax and let the behavior come naturally. You do have to stay diligent to get the job done thought. If your child is not toilet trained by school age, limitations may be set for opportunities for education and further socialization.

One method is to watch what your child does before they soil themselves. Write down a list of what they do and when they do it. If you realize that your child gets up in the morning and drinks a glass of juice and twenty minutes later they soil themselves, then you have something to work with. If the child goes through the same routine, you can put the child on the toilet during the time they normally soil themselves and see what happens. Once you get the morning soiling scheduled, add on an afternoon and evening. Pretty soon the body will work out the system even though the child does not. It is repeated, routine behavior and eventually the child will be bought in.

Does this sound like a lot of hard work? It is. Even parents of non-autistic children stress and labor over potty training their child. Each parent will give you a different bit of advice about what worked for them, but you as a parent of an autistic child know what extra you are in for. Be patient. Try different methods and remember that you have probably never seen a teenage in pampers. It takes time and patience.

Difficulties of an Autistic Adult

That's right, autistic kids grow up. This entire text has been devoted to the autistic child, but what about autistic adults? What kinds of difficulties do autistic adults have when they are in our society, at the workplace, or raising a family of their own?

Many autistic adults work, go to school, and live a semi-normal life. There are autistic professors at universities, autistic doctors, and there are some autistic adults that work at Burger King. Remember each autistic person is an individual and has different abilities according to their autism.

One of the challenges the autistic adults have the face is assumptions about their ability to do a task. An employer or co-worker will not assign a specific work related task to an autistic adult employee because it is assumed that they cannot do the task or will not do it correctly. These assumptions are picked up by the autistic adult and emotional pain is felt when they are judged by their peers. They have a want and a right to try any task that is put before another peer and not be prejudged.

The world also has trouble with the autistic adult not being able to initiate a conversation or other social interaction. Most autistic adults have trouble giving eye contact and in the work place there are people that do not understand this and will be offended because of it. Shaking hands and other social gestures are sometimes difficult for them. Some adults will even avoid using the bathroom because the interaction in a closed public restroom is to much for them to bear. The employer should be educated on the behaviors of their autistic employee and precautions should be put in place to avoid embarrassment and miscommunication.

Hygiene is another problem for the autistic adult. Some autistic adults have a hard time combing their hair or brushing their teeth. Sensitivity in these areas cause them to avoid grooming or bathing all together. Some avoid and some just give up. They know they have problems and after awhile it is easier to ignore them than to face them at all. Simple chores like laundry may be ignored and the employees and other adults in the workplace can make some pretty cruel comments about the cleanliness of the adult.

Eating and nutrition are sometimes a problem for the autistic adult. They will refuse any food that offends their senses or gives them a bad feeling. Sometimes they will not know how to prepare food and will eat less nutritious foods in substitute. The act of deciding what too much food is and what is to little is another issue. Sometimes an autistic adult will gorge themselves when eating, while another individual will eat just enough to stay alive. Some autistic adults have quirks about what and how they eat.

Foods sometimes need to be separated from other foods or a mixture of foods will cause a bad reaction.

If you have an autistic child that is an adult or you are an autistic adult reading this, the only way that the uninformed public to understand what autism is and how it affects the individual is awareness and education. Hopefully the world will learn and understand the special nature of an autistic child and adult and they can embrace the uniqueness and understand their issues.

Alternative Treatments for Autism

As with most disorders and diseases there is always a claim from doctors that there is an alternative treatment. These claims can not go unchecked. The doctors who have tried alternative treatments may have found success and the treatment has just not gone through proper channels to be approved. If you are a parent of an autistic child, you might want to check into alternative treatments. If there is any chance of success or improvement in your child's ability to communicate better or to have better social skills there is no harm in giving it a try.

One alternative treatment is the use of nalrexone. Nalrexone has had a few reports of the positive change it has made in some autistic patience. Remember there are levels of autism and the results for one child will be just about as individualized as the disorder. Nalrexone blocks the actions of the endogenous opioids which are like the endorphins that give pleasure to the brain. Research has shown that some autistic children have a high concentration of these endorphins in their brain. The improvements noted by observers of children with autism on nalrexone have included increased eye contact, better social skills, and reduction of clumsy behavior that could lead to self-injury.

When trying to use behavior altering drugs on an autistic child, you really have to look at the side effects associated with the medication. The side effects sometimes outweigh the benefits. The autistic child is wired differently than most patients. The child may need higher dosages of medication that can cause dramatic changes in their liver functions or other vital organs. The medications may have to be monitored and the dosages changed to get the desired behavior changes. More blood and lab work will have to be done to make sure that the medications are not damaging any other tissue.

The opposite might be true. People with autism have a more sensitive nervous system than most people. A lower dosage might be required, where a high dosage would overload the nervous system and have severe emotional and physical consequences. A good indicator that your child has to high of a dose of medication is that he or she will get up earlier in the morning. If this happens consult with your doctor and reduce the dosage.

Another treatment that may be unconventional is the use of acupuncture. Even those skilled in this Chinese treatment state that autism is non-curable. They do say that when they have treated autistic children with acupuncture, the parents report slight improvement. The acupuncturists theorize that the benefit comes from the neurons that the needles stimulate in the brain. There have been no research regarding acupuncture and autism and the only reports have been the ones from parents. Again, most parents are looking for anything that helps and sometimes the improvements are real and sometimes they are just manifestations of false hope.

As with any new treatment, you should consult with your doctor or your team of professionals that are already assembled to help your child through treatment. Trying alternative methods and medicines alone can set up both you and your child for failure.

About The Author

Shelley Lewis is a working mother as well as a writer. Her aim is to help as many parents as she could in rearing their ADHD child. She has created many materials in the hope to have a healthy relationship within family members.

Shelley also conducted many workshops for parents and teachers of kids with ADHD/ADD. She lives in Ohio with her lovely daughter.

www.ingramcontent.com/pod-product-compliance
Lightning Source LLC
Chambersburg PA
CBHW050653250726
48662CB00002B/643